0 804359

ON LINE

W9-BXO-997

JBIOG
Winfr
Alter, Judy.

Oprah Winfrey /

21st Century Skills Library

Century
Skills Library

LIFE SKILLS BIOGRAPHIES

OPRAH WINFREY

Judy Alter

Cherry Lake Publishing
Ann Arbor, Michigan

Published in the United States of America by Cherry Lake Publishing
Ann Arbor, MI
www.cherrylakepublishing.com

Content Adviser: P. David Marshall, PhD, Professor and Chair of Communication
Studies, Northeastern University, Boston, Massachusetts

Photo Credits: Cover and page 1, © Nancy Kaszerman/Zuma/Corbis; page 5,
© Richard Hamilton Smith/Corbis; page 10, © Katy Winn/Corbis; pages 13, 16, and 36
© Bettmann/Corbis; page 20, © Trapper Frank/Corbis Sygma; page 23, © Corbis Sygma;
page 24, © Time & Life Pictures/Getty Images; page 27, © Deborah Feingold/Corbis;
page 28, © Mitchell Gerber/Corbis; page 30, © Hubert Boesl/dpa/Corbis; page 33,
© Corbis; page 34, © Reuters/Corbis; page 39, © Siphiwe Sibeko/Reuters/Corbis;
page 40, © Kim Ludbrook/epa/Corbis; page 42, © Chris Pizzello/Corbis

Library of Congress Cataloging-in-Publication Data
Alter, Judy, 1938–
  Oprah Winfrey / by Judith Alter.
    p. cm. — (Life skills biographies)
  ISBN-13: 978-1-60279-069-8
  ISBN-10: 1-60279-069-8
  1. Winfrey, Oprah—Juvenile literature. 2. Television personalities—United States—Biography—
Juvenile literature. 3. Actors—United States—Biography—Juvenile literature. I. Title. II. Series.
  PN1992.4.W56A78 2007
  791.4502'8092—dc22
  [B]   2007004665

Cherry Lake Publishing would like to acknowledge the work of
The Partnership for 21st Century Skills.

TABLE OF CONTENTS

INTRODUCTION

Oprah Winfrey proves a belief that Americans hold dear: that in this land of opportunity, anyone who is determined and courageous can be a success. Winfrey's story is a true rags-to-riches one. She was born on a poor farm in rural Mississippi with little hope for a future any different from her grandparents' **hardscrabble** life. She became the first African American woman to host a national TV show and is the host of the highest-rated talk show on television. *The Oprah Winfrey Show* is seen in more than a hundred countries by tens of millions of viewers. Winfrey is also a movie actress, a publisher, an **entrepreneur**, and an author. With a net worth of more than a billion dollars, she is the richest African American of the twentieth century. She is also one of the world's most generous **philanthropists**.

In her climb to success, Winfrey faced obstacles that many Americans face—poverty, a **dysfunctional** family, sexual abuse, problems with drugs, struggles with weight. The fact that she could overcome these problems illustrates her strongly held belief that "You are your possibilities."

CHAPTER ONE

HUMBLE BEGINNINGS

Oprah was born on a farm in rural Mississippi.

Oprah Gail Winfrey was born January 29, 1954, on a farm outside Kosciusko, Mississippi. She was to be named Orpah, after a woman in the story of Ruth in the Old Testament, but has always been known as Oprah. She explains that the people around her were uneducated and didn't know how to pronounce Orpah.

Oprah is the great-great-granddaughter of Mississippi slaves who were freed after the Civil War. Her mother, Vernita Lee, and her father, Vernon Winfrey, were not married. Vernita lived on the farm with her parents, and Vernon was a soldier stationed nearby. Oprah's parents did not stay together, and she was raised in her early years by her grandparents. Oprah does not remember her mother as a part of her very early childhood, but apparently Vernita stayed on the farm for a few years after Oprah's birth. Then she went North in search of a better life.

Oprah remembers being surrounded by aunts and uncles when she was young and that her grandfather Earless (pronounced Ur-liss) Lee was strict—she was a bit afraid of him. Her grandmother, Hattie Mae, was also strict. She believed "Spare the rod and spoil the child," and when Oprah misbehaved, she was sent to cut a small branch from a tree so that her grandmother could give her a switching. Her grandmother was a positive influence on Oprah, encouraging her to learn.

Oprah's grandmother had little education, but she taught her granddaughter to read by the time she was three and started her on her lifelong love of books. With her grandmother, Oprah read the Bible. Hattie Mae also taught the child to add, subtract, and write. "I am what I am because of my grandmother," Oprah has said.

On their small farm, the Lees raised chickens, turkeys, pigs, and cows and grew their own vegetables. Oprah helped care for the animals, hung out laundry, made homemade soap from lye, and drew water from a well. There was no indoor plumbing and no radio or television. Her only toy was a doll her grandmother made from a corncob. There was no money for store-bought toys. There were no neighbors nearby. Later in life, when Oprah's close friend Gayle King visited Kosciusko, she was amazed. "I knew she was poor," she said, "but I thought she lived in a neighborhood. Maybe not the best of neighborhoods, but a neighborhood." Commenting on the lack of neighbors on the dirt road, she said, "The trees really were her friends."

In response Oprah quipped, "I was po'! That's when you're so poor you can't afford the last two letters of the word." But she said that at the time she didn't know she was poor. She thought her family lived the way everyone lived.

Learning & Innovation Skills

Oprah clearly remembers one day when she was about four years old watching her grandmother boil clothes to clean them because there was no washing machine. As she watched, she thought, "My life won't be like this. It will be better." She can't explain how she knew that but says it was just a deep, sure knowledge. Her ability to see outside of her situation at such an early age hinted at her creative and inventive mind.

Already comfortable speaking in front of others at a young age, Oprah began reciting speeches in church when she was three. The preacher would introduce her, saying, "Little Mistress Winfrey will render a recitation." She heard the women of the church say she was gifted. And though she didn't know what the word meant, the women's comments made her feel special. She thinks her broadcasting career started in church.

Milwaukee, Wisconsin, is more than 750 miles (1,207 kilometers) from Oprah's hometown.

LIFE AWAY FROM THE FARM

When she was six, Oprah was sent to Milwaukee to live with her mother. Milwaukee was a large, crowded, noisy city with many businesses and factories. It must have been a shock after the quiet of rural Mississippi. But Oprah's mother did not help make the adjustment easy. When Oprah arrived, she discovered she had a younger half-sister, Patricia, whom she had to help take care of and whom she fought with all the years she was in Milwaukee. A baby brother was born later, although her mother never married. The family lived in a boardinghouse and then a small apartment, and Vernita Lee worked hard to provide for her children. Oprah says they were poor but at least they didn't live in the **projects**. Because she knew no other way, she simply accepted that was how life was and adapted to her new environment.

But Vernita was apparently not a nurturing and loving mother to Oprah. As a young girl, Oprah always felt the younger children were Vernita's favorites, perhaps because their skin was lighter than hers. Her mother did not appreciate Oprah's love of books. She refused to take her to the library and once grabbed a book away from Oprah. She said that books made Oprah think she was better than the other children.

Oprah learned early to take initiative and be **assertive**. She was bored in kindergarten and wrote the teacher a note asking to be moved to first grade. The teacher agreed.

Vernon Winfrey had a positive influence on his daughter, especially in her teen years.

When Oprah was eight, she was sent to stay with her father for the first time, in Nashville. He had married a woman named Zelma, and he held two jobs as a janitor—one at Vanderbilt University and one in a hospital. The Winfreys were childless, and they welcomed Oprah. They lived in a neat, clean house, and Oprah had a bedroom all to herself. Her father and stepmother encouraged her to read and took her to the library. They also took her to church. When they discovered she could speak and recite, they took her to churches all over Nashville to recite Bible verses and poetry. After staying with the Winfreys for a year, she returned to Milwaukee to visit her mother, initially just for the summer, but she decided to stay.

The year of Oprah's birth was the year the Supreme Court outlawed **segregation** in schools. Restrooms, drinking fountains, buses, and many other public facilities were still segregated. Oprah attended school with whites and African Americans. In third grade, she figured out that being the smartest in the class was where she felt most comfortable. She read assignments early and turned in papers ahead of time.

Her fourth-grade teacher, Mrs. Duncan, was a role model for her. Oprah has said that if she weren't doing what she is now, she'd be teaching fourth grade. Before knowing Mrs. Duncan, she had wanted to be a missionary. Oprah recalls that it was in the fourth grade that she first began to believe in herself and to believe that she could do almost anything.

In seventh grade in Milwaukee, another teacher recognized her abilities and put her in the Upward Bound program. To participate in this program, she transferred to a school in a wealthy Milwaukee suburb. She had to take three buses to get there. For the first time, she saw how others lived, and she realized that her family was poor. She was the only African American in the school, and though the other kids were friendly, she wasn't sure if they were

In school, other children teased Oprah because she was smarter than they were and liked schoolwork. They called her "Preacher" because of her recitations. But Oprah remained focused on her education, knowing that she had the ability to help define her future.

truly her friends. In the late 1960s, it was "cool" for a white person to know someone black.

TROUBLES AT HOME

If school was an inspiration, her home life got steadily worse. She longed for attention. Of the girls she now helps in Africa, she says, "They've never been told they are pretty or have wonderful dimples." Oprah "wanted to hear those things as a child." She began to misbehave as a way of getting attention. She lied to her mother, skipped school, dated lots of boys, and stole. Once she claimed their house had been robbed, smashing her glasses and stealing her mother's purse to back up her story— all because she wanted new eyeglasses.

But there was an even darker side to her home life. She was raped by a cousin when she was nine, later by a family friend, and then a favorite uncle. She even accepted this abuse as the way life was.

After Oprah attempted to run away at the age of thirteen, her mother sent her to a juvenile detention home. But she was turned away because all the beds were filled. Vernita Lee once again sent Oprah to her father in Nashville.

Oprah attended public schools in the first decade after segregation was banned.

CHANGING HER FOCUS

By then, Vernon Winfrey had established a barber-shop in Nashville. He turned out to be a strict disciplinarian—he knew she was capable and simply needed high standards and rules in her life.

As a child, Oprah was searching for love and affection and attention, and some men took advantage of that. She "unconsciously blamed [herself] for those men's acts" and now recognizes that she was not to blame. She deals with the subject of abuse on her show and counsels children in schools and other settings to share what she has learned.

Oprah's father once told her there were three kinds of people: those that make things happen, those that watch things happen, and those that don't know what's happening. She knew she wanted to be in the first group, among the leaders.

Nashville, Tennessee, is on the banks of the Cumberland River.

In addition to her schoolwork, Oprah was expected to read and report on a book a week. If she wanted dinner, she had to learn five new vocabulary words a day. She was told not to bring Cs into the house because her father knew she was an A student. And she never lied to him, because she knew that, too, was unacceptable. She has said that her father's guidance, structure, rules, and books saved her life.

She attended East High School in the early years of integration, when blacks and whites were starting to share classrooms. But people liked her, and she was elected Most Popular Girl in her class.

In Nashville, she spoke to church groups. She talked about slavery and women's rights and African American issues. She won speaking contests. After she delivered a speech titled, "The Negro, the Constitution, and the United States" to 10,000 Elks Club members in Pennsylvania, she won a $1,000 college scholarship.

Life & Career Skills

A former boyfriend remembers that Oprah "knew what she wanted very early in life. . . . She wanted to be a movie star . . . [and] an actress," and she was willing to put other things aside to achieve her goals.

CHAPTER TWO

SUCCESS IN THE CLASSROOM AND BEYOND

Oprah Winfrey's first broadcasts were on the radio, but before she turned 20 years old, she was on television.

The year 1971 was a time of many changes for Oprah Winfrey. She was chosen as one of two high school students from the state to represent Tennessee at a national White House Conference on Youth in Estes Park, Colorado. Prior to attending it, she was interviewed by Nashville radio station WVOL. The station liked the way she sounded on radio and hired her to read the news for $100 a week. Then someone at the station suggested she enter Nashville's Miss Fire Prevention contest. She remembers competing against a lot of red-haired girls and being very relaxed because she knew she wouldn't win. During the competition, each contestant was asked what she would do if she had a million dollars. While other girls were citing generous goals, such as buying automobiles for relatives and helping the poor, Winfrey said, "I would be a spendin' fool." The judges were impressed with her humor and intelligence, and she won. The same year, she was named Miss Black Tennessee and went to the Miss Black America contest. She didn't win, but the experience gave her great self-confidence.

That fall, Winfrey began attending Tennessee State University, where she majored in speech communications and performing arts. She explains her career choice by pointing out that some people are known for singing; she was known for talking. By the time she entered college, she really wanted to be an actress, but her father disapproved. He thought actresses were not worthy of respect and that if Winfrey became an actress, she would not be able to take care of herself later in life.

Winfrey's college years were sometimes a struggle. Tennessee State was a black school, and most of the students were angry about civil rights issues. They were involved in a movement called Black Power, which focused on gaining more power for black citizens through political activism and sometimes violence. Because she wasn't outraged by her treatment as an African American, other students called her an "Oreo"— black on the outside and white on the inside. She was not concerned. Her life began in the afternoons when she went to work at the radio station.

In her sophomore year, she was asked by WTVF-TV, a Nashville television station and local CBS **affiliate**, if she'd be interested in reading

the news on the air. She refused several times, but her speech teacher reminded her that such job offers are "the reason many people go to college," so she auditioned. During the audition, having never been in front of a television camera, she said she pretended she was Barbara Walters (a pioneering journalist who was the first female anchor on an evening news broadcast). She was hired, and at age nineteen, she became a reporter and coanchor for the evening news—and the first black woman to read the news on TV in Nashville. She was paid $15,000 a year. In spite of her heavy work schedule, Winfrey finished college and graduated in 1976.

Looking back on the experience, she has said that she thinks she was hired because of the times. There had been bad race riots in America, and businesses were eager to hire minorities in an effort to smooth over the troubles and abide by Affirmative Action laws—guidelines that the government had introduced to encourage diversity. She was black and she was female, and, she admits, she was a token. When classmates at her all-black college taunted her, she said, "Yeah, but I'm a *paid* token."

CHAPTER THREE

CAREER ADVANCEMENT

Oprah Winfrey called Baltimore, Maryland, home for seven years.

In 1976, Winfrey moved to Baltimore to become a reporter and coanchor for the ABC affiliate WJZ-TV. She told the station manager she knew how to report on stories—but she didn't. She said she knew how to edit—but she didn't. When she went to her first city council meeting, she walked in and told them it was her first day, she didn't know what she was doing, and would they please help her. The council members did, and from then on they were her friends. She attributes this to her willingness to admit what

Phil Donahue hosted his own talk show on national television for 27 years.

she doesn't know and ask for help. She was not, however, a good news reporter because she got too emotionally involved to go after the story. If a mother had just lost a child in a fire, Winfrey wouldn't disturb her grief to interview her. The station manager would ask, "What do you mean you didn't talk to her?" She was moved from evening coanchor to a spot on the 5:30 AM news, a definite downgrade.

The station also tried to change her appearance. They sent her to a New York salon, where a beautician left straightening chemicals on her hair too long, and it fell out. She had to wear wigs. They sent her for voice and **diction** lessons, but the voice coach said there was nothing wrong with her voice. She just needed to learn to speak up. Winfrey wondered if the studio was trying to make her into a white person.

She had a contract, so the station could not fire her. But they moved her again. She became cohost of *Baltimore Is Talking*, a morning talk show, in 1977. On her first show, she interviewed Tom Carvel, the founder of Carvel Ice Cream, and an actor from the TV soap *All My Children*. "I came off the air, thinking, 'This is what I should have been doing,'" she has said. "It was like breathing to me. . . . You just talk." Her style was conversational, friendly, and sometimes emotional—much better suited to a talk show than to straight news reporting. She gave new life to the show, and *Baltimore Is Talking* went on to beat Phil Donahue's popular national talk show in local markets. (Donahue is generally considered the inventor of the tabloid talk show, a program where the host asks audience members what they think about the show's topic.)

Winfrey was in Baltimore for seven years. By 1983, she wanted her own show. And in 1984, ABC affiliate WLS-TV in Chicago hired her to take over a morning talk show, *A.M. Chicago*, which had low ratings. Once again, she gave life to a humdrum show, this time by focusing on current and controversial topics—sibling rivalry, wife battering, children of divorce. She interviewed ordinary people, talked about subjects that affected their lives, and shared her own difficult personal stories. Within a month, she pulled the ratings up until she was

On his daytime talk show, Phil Donahue tended to focus on issues that were often controversial, such as abortion, civil rights, consumer protection, and war protests. Winfrey tends to focus on people's feelings about an issue. Her audience appreciated her ability to connect with them.

even with Donahue, the rival who had become her measure of success. In 1985, the show was given a full hour and renamed *The Oprah Winfrey Show*.

VENTURING INTO MOVIES

Even as she was building her TV show's reputation, Winfrey moved her career in another direction. She was fascinated by Alice Walker's novel *The Color Purple*, about a black woman in the South who writes letters to God about her life. When Winfrey heard that it was going to be made into a movie, she wanted to be part of it, though she had no idea how to do that. Quincy Jones, one of the coproducers, was in Chicago briefly, saw Winfrey on TV, and thought she'd be perfect as Sofia. (Sofia was a secondary character in the book, a woman determined to take charge of her own life in spite of an abusive husband.) Jones contacted Winfrey, who auditioned for the role and got it. She took time away from her show to film the movie, which later won her nominations for an Academy Award and a Golden Globe in the Best Supporting Actress category. *The Color Purple*, which opened in theaters on December 18, 1985, also made her a national star.

Winfrey starred in the movie Beloved, *which premiered in 1998.*

In 1986, she had a major role in *Native Son*, a film based on a book by African American novelist Richard Wright. That year, she established her **production company**, Harpo (Oprah spelled backward), and two years later, she bought her own studio. Her company produces television shows and movies, *O, The Oprah Magazine*, and online sites. One of her goals is to bring more people of color into the film and television industry. Over the years, she has purchased the film rights to several books that have interested her, including Toni Morrison's *Beloved*. She felt as strongly about *Beloved* as she had about *The Color Purple* and starred in the film, which took her ten years to make. It was not a box-office success, which was a major disappointment to her.

Winfrey starred in There Are No Children Here, *which was shot in Chicago.*

In the late 1980s, her production company, now called Harpo Productions, bought *The Oprah Winfrey Show* from ABC. Winfrey finally had control of her own show. The company has continued to produce television shows, including *The Women of Brewster Place* and *There Are No Children Here*, about black families in a Chicago housing project.

CHANGING SUBJECTS

In its early years, *The Oprah Winfrey Show* featured **sensational** subjects, but Winfrey realized that she couldn't do the kind of show other people did. In the midst of a show with white supremacists, she thought, "This is doing nobody any good, nobody." Now she is careful about the topics she chooses. She will not give racists a place to air their views, nor will she do a show on Satan worship. Once she taped a show about a serial killer and interviewed the families of some of his victims. But, again, she thought the show would not help anyone, so she never aired it. As Winfrey led the show in a different direction, her audience followed.

In the late 1990s, Winfrey changed the focus of her program and called the new theme for the show "Change Your Life TV." She would do programs that helped people lead happier lives, learn to understand themselves better, and change their bad habits. She believes that as an African American, she comes from people who have had no voice, and she has been given the opportunity to speak and to make a difference in people's lives.

As an example of her desire to help people, in 2004, she held a car giveaway on the air. Pontiac gave an automobile to each of the 276 people in the audience. Winfrey had made sure the audience was loaded with people who desperately needed cars.

Some of her shows have caused controversy—and one led to a lawsuit. In 1996, she did a show about **mad cow disease**. Listening to the expert who was talking about the epidemic then sweeping Britain, Winfrey swore she would never eat another hamburger. Several cattlemen in Texas banded together to file a lawsuit in Amarillo against her and Harpo for damage to the cattle industry. They claimed that cattle prices dropped dramatically after the show aired. Winfrey moved the entire show to Amarillo, while she fought in court for her rights to freedom of speech. She won the case and was cheered when she emerged triumphant from the courthouse.

She has been accused of being controlling about her show, but she says she wants the show to reflect her personality and interests. To do a show that she isn't interested in would be phony, according to her. Consequently, she is assertive about what projects she will do, and she has the final say. She wants guests who are self-revealing, and she likes to think of her show as a casual conversation. But as the host, she will go after the facts.

Although she has done many shows that confront issues, she has also done lighthearted shows with people such as Hillary Clinton, Michael Jackson, Tiger Woods, Barbara Walters, Michael Jordan, and the Duchess of York, Sarah Ferguson.

OBSESSION WITH WEIGHT LOSS

Over the years, diet and weight control have been big subjects on Winfrey's show. She had fought a weight problem since her days in Baltimore when she was lonely and poor. She found that junk food—especially corn dogs and chocolate chip cookies—was a great comfort. When she moved to Chicago, she tried to remake herself, dieting to meet what she saw as the current standard of femininity. But she continued to go from dieting to overeating to weight gain and back and forth.

In 1988, she lost 67 pounds (30 kilograms) in about four months on a liquid diet. On her first show devoted to her own weight loss, she paraded onstage wearing size 10 Calvin Klein jeans and revealing her new, trimmer shape. The show was one of the highest rated to date. But within one year, she had gained all her weight back, which is not unusual when someone loses a dramatic amount of weight in a short time. In the following years,

Bob Greene has written several books about fitness and eating right.

When Winfrey weighed 237 pounds, Bob Greene said to her, "How much do you love yourself?" She thought she loved herself; she thought she believed in taking care of herself first. But she realized she cared more about everyone else's feelings than her own and that she needed to adjust her mindset, seeing that mental well being is essential for true health and wellness.

she lost and gained weight several times. Her physical image became her measure of success. She was obsessed with weight loss.

Things changed when she met personal trainer Bob Greene. He asked her why she was overweight, which she thought was a dumb question. But finally she realized she ate not for the food but for comfort. She was doing shows that dealt with difficult topics—divorce and abuse. She was in a competitive

In 1994, Winfrey ran a **marathon** in Washington, D.C. She finished in four hours, twenty-nine minutes, and twenty seconds—not bad time for a woman running her first marathon. Completing the marathon showed her competitive spirit and determination.

business. There were many demands on her for money. She was able to give her mother, father, and a cousin enough money to retire, but people were constantly asking for her money and help. She finally learned to say no. But still she ate. When she was up for an Emmy Award in 1992, she prayed Phil Donahue would win so she wouldn't have to display her weight walking onstage.

As Greene began to help her work through the feelings she was hiding—guilt over whom to support, her suspicion that she was doing sensational

Winfrey and Greene participated in a walk held on Mother's Day in New York City.

shows—she began to take unhealthy foods out of her life. More important, she concentrated less on weight gain and more on a healthy lifestyle. Today, she eats smaller portions of healthful foods as a way of life, not as a diet that she will eventually go off, and she exercises on a fairly regular basis. Staying healthy, she firmly believes, is the most important way of taking care of yourself. Winfrey coauthored a book on healthy living with Greene, *Make the Connection: Ten Steps to a Better Body—And a Better You.*

RECOMMENDING BOOKS

In a first for talk shows, Winfrey began a book club in 1996. She chose eight or nine books a year that she liked, discussed them on the air, and brought their authors on the show when possible. Viewers across the country read the books, and their sales soared. America was reading, and booksellers were delighted. Sometimes she chose new titles that might not otherwise have gained a wide audience—such as her first choice, *The Deep End of the Ocean* by Jacquelyn Mitchard, a novel about a child's kidnapping and its effect on his family, or *White Oleander* by Janet Fitch, about a teenager whose mother goes to jail, leaving her to care for herself. But Winfrey was just as likely to choose classics—*As I Lay Dying* and *The Sound and the Fury* by William Faulkner were on her list, as were Alan Paton's *Cry, the Beloved Country* and Pearl Buck's *The Good Earth.*

After 2002, her choices became less frequent. One book she recommended in 2005 led to one of her most memorable shows. It was James Frey's *A Million Little Pieces*, about the author's dark experiences with drugs and alcohol addiction. After Winfrey had recommended the

Sidney Poitier, an award-winning actor, is credited with breaking the color barrier in the film industry in the United States.

book to her viewers and Frey had appeared on the show, it came out that Frey had made up some parts of the story. Since he claimed to be writing a memoir, and not fiction, Winfrey was outraged. She called him back on the show and told him without sympathy that he betrayed millions of readers. The show featured Winfrey at her angriest and her most honest—telling viewers that she had been wrong and those who questioned her were right. The truth, she said, always matters.

In January 2007, she announced her first book choice since the James Frey upset. Her choice this time was *The Measure of a Man*, by her good friend Sidney Poitier.

BEYOND THE TALK SHOW

Winfrey has not been content with her high-ranking TV show. She teamed with other powerful women in TV to launch Oxygen Media, a cable network and Internet company that debuted in 1998 with programming for women. She created a series, *Oprah Goes Online*, describing her adventures as she tried to become computer literate. She also taught briefly at Northwestern University in the Graduate School of Management but found that the course load was too much for her schedule. She joined with a Chicago restaurant corporation to operate a restaurant, The Eccentric, for several years.

In 2000, Winfrey launched a women's magazine called O, *The Oprah Magazine.* It contains articles on self-improvement, with topics such as fitness, quitting smoking, makeovers, finances, personal growth, and relationships. There are recipes and usually pieces by Winfrey, perhaps about coming to terms with an overeating lifestyle. In one issue, singer Josh Groban wrote about how miserable he was in high school and how he learned the lesson of "This too shall pass." It's Winfrey's philosophy at its best.

Oprah.com is one of the most popular women's lifestyle Web sites. It offers everything from clips of various shows to advice for both men and women to a segment called "Oprah After the Show," in which she talks informally with guests and the audience, following whatever direction the audience's questions and comments take her. The site includes lists of Winfrey's book choices, excerpts from the magazine, recipes, and a section advertising the kind of guests Winfrey wants for future shows—questions like "Have a Romantic Story?" or "Is Your House Stuck in a Time Warp?"

Her business empire is complicated, but Winfrey runs it with a tight hand. She is chairman and CEO (chief executive officer) and surrounds herself with people she trusts and feels are smarter than she is, so that she can learn from them. She feels a responsibility to know as much about her business as she can. She works twelve-to-fifteen-hour days. If she goes home early, she wonders what to do with the rest of her day. If she goes home late, she takes a bubble bath and goes to bed with a pile of books, papers, and magazines.

AWARDS AND OTHER SUCCESSES

By all ordinary measurements, Winfrey has achieved great success. In 1986, the Chicago Academy for the Arts gave her a special award for contributions to the city's artistic community. That same year, the National Organization for Women named her Woman of Achievement. In 1987, the first year that *The Oprah Winfrey Show* was eligible for the Emmy Awards, the show won awards for Outstanding Talk/Service Program and Outstanding Direction, and she was honored as Best Talk Show Host. Both she and the program have since won several more times.

In 1993, she won the Horatio Alger Award, for those who overcome difficulties to become outstanding in their chosen field of work. She was inducted into the Television Hall of Fame in 1994 and won broadcasting's George Foster Peabody Individual Achievement Award in 1996. Also in 1996, she received a Gold Medal Award from the International Radio and Television

Society, the youngest person and only the fifth woman to be so honored. That year, *Time* magazine named her one of America's 25 Most Influential People, and she was also included on a list of the most polite celebrities. In 1997, she was *TV Guide*'s Television Performer of the Year and won the People's Choice Award for Female Television Performer. In 1998, *Entertainment Weekly* named her the most powerful person in show business.

Winfrey's success has allowed her much financial freedom. She owns estates outside Santa Barbara,

Many people are inspired by Winfrey. In a 2006 poll conducted by the Associated Press/AOL, 29 percent named Winfrey the best role model—the highest rating of anyone in the survey. Three percent called her the biggest hero of the year.

Winfrey won her first Emmy in 1987.

Winfrey and Stedman Graham have been together for more than 20 years.

California, and on an island off the Florida coast; property in Hawaii; a ski lodge in Telluride, Colorado; a house in New Jersey; and an apartment in Chicago. She also has a private jet, several luxury automobiles, an extensive wardrobe, and an expensive jewelry collection. While she is not embarrassed about her wealth, neither does she believe it defines her: "Though I am grateful for the blessings of wealth, it hasn't changed who I am. My feet are still on the ground. I'm just wearing better shoes." She would be doing what she's doing, she has said, without pay.

On the air, Winfrey is **candid** and sometimes brutally frank about her life. In 1995, she told a startled audience that she had smoked cocaine when she was working—and miserable—in Baltimore. She did it, she said, for a boyfriend about whom she desperately cared; she now thinks of the act as her "great shame." But if she is open about her past, she is very private about her life today. Employees of Harpo Productions are forbidden to write or talk about her or the company for the rest of their lives.

Winfrey, however, cannot avoid the publicity that reveals she is the pal and companion of the rich and famous. She celebrated her fiftieth birthday at a lavish party in Santa Barbara, hosted by good friends. The guests included famous people from all walks of life but mostly movie stars. Winfrey counts poet Maya Angelou as a dear friend and closely identifies with Angelou's memoir, *I Know Why the Caged Bird Sings.* In that book, Angelou tells of her early childhood. She too lived with her grandmother in the South and later with her mother and then her father. She was raped as a child and, like Winfrey, found comfort in books.

Winfrey has been blessed with two continuing presences in her life. One is Stedman Graham Jr., her companion since 1986. An entrepreneur, motivational speaker, author, and founder of Athletes Against Drugs, Graham heads S. Graham and Associates, a management and marketing consultant firm. Like Winfrey, he is committed to youth and the community.

When she was working at WJZ in Baltimore, Winfrey met Gayle King, who also worked at the station. One night during a blizzard, Winfrey invited King to spend the night since she lived close to the station. The two stayed up all night talking, and they've been talking ever since, sometimes three or four times a day. Today, King frequently travels with Winfrey, accompanying her to South Africa several times, and King is editor-at-large of *O, The Oprah Magazine.*

CHAPTER FOUR

GIVING BACK TO THE COMMUNITY

Winfrey was emotional during her testimony before a Senate committee in 1991.

Winfrey's success has allowed her to become an influential advocate for a number of causes. In 1987, she established the Oprah Winfrey Foundation for the education and empowerment of women, children, and families. The foundation focuses on education and health care. She established scholarships to Tennessee State University in her father's name and contributes to that program annually. In 1989, she gave $1 million to Morehouse College. She has made generous contributions to the Chicago Public Library Foundation and the United Negro College Fund, among others.

After hearing the story of a four-year-old Chicago girl who was abused and murdered, Winfrey campaigned to establish a national database of convicted child abusers. She testified before a Senate committee for the National Child Protection Act, soon known as the Oprah Bill, and President Bill Clinton signed it into law in 1993. It allows child care providers to check the background of all prospective employees and guarantees strict sentencing for people convicted of child abuse. No doubt Winfrey had her own childhood experiences in mind as she fought for this legislation.

On her September 18, 1997, show, Winfrey invited the audience to join her in using their lives to improve the lives of others. First, she asked Americans to donate their spare change to college scholarships to be administered through Boys and Girls Clubs of America. She raised more than $3 million and sent 150 kids to college. Next she asked people to volunteer time to build 200 homes for

Life & Career Skills

Morehouse College in Atlanta, Georgia, is the only all-male, traditionally black institution of higher learning in the United States. Winfrey's contributions to it exemplify her interest in helping others.

Habitat for Humanity, the organization that builds houses for the poor.

Oprah's Angel Network was formed as a public charity in 1998, and gifts to it are tax deductible. The network gives out "Use Your Life" awards of $100,000 annually on the television show. The awards go to people who use their lives to help others. Currently, the network is building rural schools in eleven underprivileged countries. Estimates are that the charity has raised more than $50 million, mostly from audience donations.

Winfrey sponsors the A Better Chance program, which helps inner-city children attend college prep schools. Her video, "Oprah: Make the Connection," is about her struggle with her weight, and proceeds go to A Better Chance.

AFRICAN SCHOOL

The project that occupies Winfrey's time, energy, and money these days is the Oprah Winfrey Leadership Academy for Girls at Henley-on-Klip, South Africa, outside Johannesburg. She has spent several years and some $40 million planning this elaborate school, which opened January 2, 2007.

*More than 3,000 girls applied to the Oprah
Winfrey Leadership Academy for Girls.*

The academy is set on 52 acres (21 hectares), with twenty-eight buildings for classrooms, a library, an amphitheater, dormitories, a gymnasium, and a dining hall. It has space for 152 girls in first-class quarters that rival a luxury resort—with fine linen bedclothes, comfortable beds for girls who before may have only slept on dirt floors, attractive green uniforms, and fine china in the dining hall.

When she started planning the academy, local architects designed simple, spare buildings, saying that South African girls were not used

South Africa is a poor country. It has been only thirteen years since the nation abandoned **apartheid**, or strict racial segregation. Violence against females is common there, and about one out of every eight people is HIV positive. Many black women are illiterate and unemployed. That's the statistic Winfrey intends to change.

Winfrey celebrates the opening of the Oprah Winfrey Leadership Academy for Girls.

to much and would be grateful. Winfrey dismissed them and hired her own architects. She wanted her school to be first class, to show girls what was possible in the world. Her belief is that these girls—chosen for their leadership qualities—can change their lives, then the country, and, eventually, the world.

For the grand opening, Winfrey arrived with a crowd of celebrities including actor Sidney Poitier, singer Mariah Carey, and actor-comedian Chris Tucker. She brought them, she said, because they had voices that would be heard in the United States and across the world.

During the opening week of the school, Winfrey very publicly took an HIV test and encouraged the students and their families to do the same. "To be a great leader," she said, "you must be of sound mind, body, and spirit." She has assured the mothers of the girls who enter the school that she will take good care of their daughters, and she refers to them as "my girls."

The academy has not been without critics. Originally, the South African government was a partner in the project, but the government was reportedly not comfortable with the elaborate nature of Winfrey's plans. She preferred to let them pull out and do it the way she wanted. She has announced plans to open a school for boys and girls in another province of South Africa soon.

Some critics wondered why she was helping girls in another country instead of the United States. Her response to such criticism: "I'm doing a lot in the United States. I just don't talk about it."

CHAPTER FIVE

FUTURE PLANS

Winfrey is the first African American woman billionaire.

Winfrey has extended her contract for *The Oprah Winfrey Show* through the 2010–11 season. She says she does not want to stay too long and that she will know when it's time to quit. But for now, the show is important because it's a "platform for being able to make a difference in people's lives." She knows, she says, that "it's not going to work forever."

She developed and is producing a talk show for celebrity chef Rachael Ray, and Winfrey is the voice of a character in the 2007 film *Bee Movie.* If her past record is any indication, she will continue to seek new projects for many years to come. She still wants to act and is no doubt looking for movie roles that suit her.

After retirement, she plans to spend time in South Africa, where she'll build a home on the grounds of the Oprah Winfrey Leadership Academy for Girls.

Winfrey once said it is easy to help individuals, but it's more important to bring change to a culture or a country. That is what she hopes she's doing in South Africa. Winfrey hopes she will leave a legacy of change, not just for individuals but for the world.

Throughout her life, in the face of many hardships, she remained focused and determined. Winfrey's story—one of success and of a life's possibilities—will certainly be part of her legacy.

Hoping to instill a sense of personal responsibility in the potential students at her academy in South Africa, she said: "You cannot blame apartheid, your parents, your circumstances, because you are not your circumstances. You are your possibilities."

TIMELINE

1954   Oprah Gail Winfrey is born January 29 in Kosciusko, Mississippi.

1960   Oprah moves to Milwaukee to live with her mother.

1968   Oprah moves to Tennessee to live with her father.

1971   Oprah is the first black woman to be Nashville's Miss Fire Prevention.

1976   Winfrey graduates from Tennessee State University with a degree in speech communication and performing arts.

1977   Winfrey becomes cohost of *Baltimore Is Talking*.

1984   Winfrey becomes host of *A.M. Chicago*.

1985   *A.M. Chicago* is changed to *The Oprah Winfrey Show* and expanded to one hour; Quincy Jones casts Winfrey in *The Color Purple*.

1986   Winfrey forms a production company, Harpo. She wins an award from the Chicago Academy for the Arts for unique contributions to the city's artistic community and is named Woman of Achievement by the National Organization for Women.

1987   *The Oprah Winfrey Show* wins three Emmys.

1993   Winfrey wins the Horatio Alger Award for those who overcame adversity to become leaders in their chosen fields.

1994   Winfrey is inducted into the Television Hall of Fame.

1996   Winfrey receives the George Foster Peabody Individual Achievement Award and the International Radio and TV Society's Gold Medal Award. She is named one of America's 25 Most Influential People by *Time* magazine.

1997   Winfrey is named *TV Guide's* Television Performer of the Year and the favorite Female Television Performer at the 1997 People's Choice Awards.

1998   Winfrey is named the most powerful person in show business by *Entertainment Weekly*. She produces the feature film, *Beloved*, and wins an Emmy for Lifetime Achievement. Oprah's Angel Network is established.

1999   Winfrey teaches a course, "Dynamics of Leadership," at Northwestern University with Stedman Graham Jr. The National Book Foundation gives her its 50th Anniversary Gold Medal for the work she had done to promote reading in the United States.

2000   Harpo launches *O, The Oprah Winfrey Magazine*. Winfrey is honored by Coretta Scott King at the Salute to Greatness Awards dinner at the King Center.

2001   Winfrey purchases an estate on the California coast. She is listed among the 10 most influential people in publishing and 280th on the *Forbes* list of the 400 richest people in America. Winfrey goes on tour with the seminar series entitled "Live Your Best Life." She cohosts a memorial service for victims of the 9/11 attacks.

2002   Winfrey is given the Bob Hope Humanitarian Award for contributions to broadcasting.

2006   Poll conducted by the Associated Press/AOL names Winfrey the best role model.

2007   The Oprah Winfrey Leadership Academy for Girls opens in South Africa.

Glossary

affiliate (uh-FIL-ee-ate) in this case, a radio or TV station that operates in close association with a national network

apartheid (uh-PART-hate) a policy of racial segregation

assertive (uh-SUR-tiv) speaking strongly and directly for what you believe and what you want

candid (KAN-did) frank, open, honest, and sincere

diction (DIK-shuhn) vocal expression

dysfunctional (diss-FUHNGK-shu-nuhl) not able to function properly, as in a family that does not support and encourage individual family members

entrepreneur (on-truh-pruh-NUR) one who successfully organizes and manages a business, usually with imagination and unusual techniques

hardscrabble (HARD-skra-buhl) marked by poverty

mad cow disease (MAD KOU duh-ZEEZ) a chronic and fatal disease affecting the nervous systems of cattle and of people who eat infected cattle

marathon (MAR-uh-thon) a foot race for 26 miles, 385 yards (42.2 kilometers)

philanthropists (fuh-LAN-thruh-pists) people who make large and frequent donations of money, land, or work for the good of mankind

production company (pruh-DUHK-shuhn KUHM-puh-nee) a company that makes movies for television or large theater screens and/or produces television shows

projects (PROJ-ekts) public low-income housing developments, often multistoried apartment buildings

segregation (seg-ruh-GAY-shuhn) separating people according to their race or religion

sensational (sen-SAY-shu-nuhl) arousing or tending to arouse a quick, intense, and usually superficial interest, curiosity, or emotional reaction

FOR MORE INFORMATION

Books

Altman, Susan. *Extraordinary African Americans.* New York: Children's Press, 2001.

Chin-Lee, Cynthia. *Amelia to Zora: Twenty-Six Women Who Changed the World.* Watertown, MA: Charlesbridge, 2005.

Cooper, Ilene. *Oprah Winfrey.* New York: Viking Juvenile, 2007.

Krohn, Katherine. *Oprah Winfrey.* Minneapolis: Lerner Publications, 2005.

Ward, Kristin. *Learning About Assertiveness from the Life of Oprah Winfrey.* New York: PowerKids Press, 1999.

Web Sites

Academy of Achievement: Oprah Winfrey
www.achievement.org/autodoc/page/win0pro-1
Features a biography, interview, and images

The Oprah Winfrey Show
www2.oprah.com/index.jhtml
Includes information about Oprah Winfrey's show, magazine, book club, and philanthropy, as well as a biography and timeline of her life

Thomson Gale: Oprah Winfrey Biography
www.gale.com/free_resources/bhm/bio/winfrey_o.htm
For an overview of Winfrey's personal life, career, and influence

INDEX

ABOUT THE AUTHOR

Judy Alter is the author of numerous books for young readers, as well as novels for young adults and adults. Recent titles include *Souvenirs from the Stars, John Barclay Armstrong: Texas Ranger,* and *Martín de Leon: Tejano Empresario.* Alter has been director of a small university press for twenty years. She is the mother of four grown children and the grandmother of seven. She lives in Fort Worth, Texas, with her Australian shepherd, Scooby, and her cat, Wynona.